More Critical Praise for David Duchovny

for *The Reservoir*

"Evocative, chilly prose that wouldn't be out of place in a late Don DeLillo novel. Like his previous novels *Bucky F*cking Dent* and *Miss Subways*, it's a love letter to Duchovny's native New York. But it's also a smart story about obsession. A slim, compelling tale of a man on the brink."   —*Kirkus Reviews*

"[C]omically absurd, funny, and very dark."   —*New York Journal of Books*

"[Duchovny's] novella *The Reservoir*, set in New York City, probes how pandemic isolation has changed us."   —*Boston Globe*

"David Duchovny's existentialist novella is not to be missed . . . It is a novel of many well-crafted and complex lines [and] Duchovny's writing is a combination of high and low—and yes, that distinction still exists, if barely. His metaphors and similes are arresting . . . *The Reservoir* is an important novel for how it captures, not just where we are now, but where we are forever. Disease—like COVID, or like tuberculosis in *The Magic Mountain*—takes us on a journey outward and at the same time inward."
—*City Journal*

"This swift and unnerving fever dream of a novella, Duchovny's fifth work of fiction, is saturated with mythic and literary allusions and shaped by resonant riffs on Poe and Mann. At once philosophical and suspenseful, grandly imaginative and sharply funny, this mind-bending story of delusion and longing is a dark reflection of New York's countless crimes and tragedies and much-tested resilience, emblematic of the suffering and tenacity of all of humanity."   —*Booklist*

"The progeny of our current pandemic is various: illness and death, of course, but also economic dislocation and personal isolation, the concept of 'social distancing' having quickly morphed from an advisory into a way of life. David Duchovny's excellent new novella, *The Reservoir*, is a fever dream born out of this isolation." —*PopMatters*

"[A] lonely ex-financier stuck in his apartment during the COVID-19 pandemic becomes obsessed with the Central Park Reservoir and slowly goes mad."
—*New York Times Book Review*

"This intelligent effort further burnishes Duchovny's status as a gifted novelist."
—*Publishers Weekly*

"David Duchovny writes like Bob Dylan, but in prose. There's irony, poetry, there's social commentary. There's a brooding outrage. And there's romance, too. The complex, multilayered novella, *The Reservoir* . . . is an easy-to-read, hard-to-forget page-turner."   —*Pavlovic Today*

"Bump [*The Reservoir*] to the top of your summer reading list immediately."
—*CultureWag*

"Biting and funny, *The Reservoir* is also deep and reflective. A mystery wrapped in a fever dream. A tale for our infectious times."

—Chris Carter, director/writer, creator of *The X-Files*

"Inspired by Duchovny's self-reflection while sequestered in his own aerie above Central Park at the height of the pandemic, this work is provocative, challenging, and not without its moments of dark humor."

—*Library Journal*

for *Truly Like Lightning*

"Duchovny is best known for his idiosyncratic roles in *The X-Files* and *Californication*, and he has a wildly unpredictable voice as a writer. Here he offers a dramatic parable involving trespasses against others and the dire consequences that follow . . . Duchovny's characteristically nimble prose not only connects the various narratives, but exposes the complicated humanity of his multifarious cast. An engrossing story about a clash of cultures and the extremities of faith."

—*Kirkus Reviews*

"A provocative, entertaining book that, much like Tom Wolfe did, exposes our collective foibles and makes everybody look a little cartoonish. But it persuades you that we deserve the caricature he's made of us."

—*Washington Post*

"This beguiling book crackles with energy and intelligence. It makes you laugh and then just when you think the ride is coming to an end . . . it delivers a right hook that leaves you aghast. It kind of broke my heart and I loved every minute of it."

—Samantha Bee

"*Truly Like Lightning* is an emotionally captivating tour de force from start to finish. David Duchovny fires on all cylinders in penning a modern-day fish-out-of-water tale . . . A true must-read for 2021."

—*San Francisco Book Review*

"A bucking ride through the twenty-first-century American West . . . Duchovny's jam-packed page-turner is just waiting for someone to snap up the film rights."

—*Publishers Weekly*

for *Miss Subways*

"Novels written by celebrities can be risky reads, but not in the hands of David Duchovny . . . who has crafted a witty and profound showstopper about ancient myths, modern New York City, and the persistence—and magic—of love . . . Read *Miss Subways* as a wonderful fantasy, an exquisite love story, or a valentine to New York City, but you can also, like Emer, look deeper."

—*San Francisco Chronicle*

"In Duchovny's third novel, *Miss Subways*, he demonstrates unequivocally that, to paraphrase the actor Chris Robinson who portrayed Dr. Rick Webber on *General Hospital*, he not only plays a novelist on TV, but is one . . . Even readers who aren't fans of the metaphysical will be captivated by the author's charming narrative and vivid exposition . . ."

—*New York Times*

"[*Miss Subways* is] rolling with zany characters and playful wit worthy of Tom Robbins and recent Thomas Pynchon. Duchovny writes Emer so genuinely that readers will either fall for her, or identify with her, or both . . . This is a rollicking underground ride."   —*USA Today*

"Fresh off a new season of the evergreen *X-Files* and a late-blooming music career, the multitalented Duchovny offers a spooky domestic drama that is equal parts Nick Hornby and Neil Gaiman . . . An entertaining, postmodern fairy tale that tests the boundaries of love and fate."   —*Kirkus Reviews*

"Emer has a dreamy side, compounded by a benign brain tumor, that makes her, and the reader, wonder whether she is hallucinating or if her reality keeps changing as she wages a battle for her right to love. Duchovny's humor and fondness for New York City enliven every page. Give this to readers willing to go on a wild ride." —*Booklist*

for *Bucky F*cking Dent*

• A *Time Out New York* Best Book of the Year

• A *Booklist* Editors' Choice Selection

"Hilarious and deeply touching . . . Not a baseball book any more than *Field of Dreams* is a baseball book, this moving, beautiful novel resonates with laughter and tears throughout."   —*USA Today*

"Like Bucky Dent himself, Duchovny hits an unexpected home run."
—*New York Times Book Review*

"If it's annoying that Mr. Duchovny, who's already a phenomenally successful and painfully good-looking actor, is also a funny and natural writer—his last book, the animal allegory *Holy Cow*, also earned high praise from skeptical critics—then at least give him some points for self-awareness. Like his character in *Californication*, Mr. Duchovny knows how he comes off and doesn't mind if you resent him. He just wants a fair shake."   —*New York Observer*

"Duchovny has hit this one out of the park . . . He does a terrific job of blending quirky and emotional writing."   —*Associated Press*

"Duchovny finds the humor and poetry in life's lost causes."
—*Entertainment Weekly*

"Duchovny's hilarious new novel hits a home run . . . As fast as it is entertaining . . . Duchovny has a place in the lineup, kind of like a light-hitting shortstop who shines in key moments."   —*Washington Post*

About Time

About Time

Poems

David Duchovny

BROOKLYN, NEW YORK
Publishing books since 1997

Published by Akashic Books
©2025 David Duchovny

ISBN: 978-1-63614-263-0
Library of Congress Control Number: 2025933495

EU Authorized Representative details:
Easy Access System Europe
Mustamäe tee 50, 10621 Tallinn, Estonia
gpsr.request@easproject.com

Akashic Books
Brooklyn, New York
Instagram, X, Facebook: AkashicBooks
info@akashicbooks.com
www.akashicbooks.com

To Margaret Emerson, James Shields, Bruce Breimer,
Maria DiBattista, and Monique Duchovny

Table of Contents

Introduction

A Poetic Autobiography

I know what you're thinking: *Just what the world needs now—a bunch of poems from an actor.*

I'm only half kidding. Poetry is lies. Poetry makes nothing happen. Plato banished poets from the perfect society because they make us feel more than think. Too much passion, not enough reason. You cannot get rich at it. It can rhyme, but it doesn't have to. People will call you a "poet" as a way of not having to deal with what you write, as if you are already dead and among those who used to try to talk like that. An unserious individual. A man out of time. Not engagé. Somehow not manly, not Teddy Roosevelt's often invoked "man in the arena." It's a doomed mission—poems try to say what can never be said. These are just a few of the virtuous things about poetry that come to mind.

Let me try to say it unpoetically. Poetry is not useful. And that is exactly why we need it. It reminds us of two important things: our ultimate lack of agency (unpopular to say, I know) and our inability to say anything plain, our inability to capture what it means to be human with the imperfect tool of words; we come face-to-face with our shadow selves, for in the end we will all die and be forgotten, and come away with nothing, nothing in the way of utility anyway, no talking points, no bullet points, no propaganda, no resolutions, no policy, no knowledge. If anything, maybe we remember a few lines, take them to heart, the lusters, or "touchstones" as Matthew Arnold called them, the greatest riffs—and they lie there modestly swaying in the seabed of our mind, barnacled and semi-ghostly; something like

13

an adult nursery rhyme, something like a pop song from the collective unconscious, something like wisdom. You see, I wanted to say it plain, but out comes that torrent of modifiers and adjustments, denials, double negatives, shading, stabs at wit, backpedaling, playing at capturing the lightning. Maybe this time. Maybe that's what a poem is—that glorious feeling of *Maybe this time I'll get it right*. If that's the case, it seems a worthy enterprise to me. You see, I got somewhere, but the way back is unclear— that's a good enough definition of poetry for now. No, it's not.

What is poetry anyway? "[T]he spontaneous overflow of powerful feelings . . . recollected in tranquility," according to Wordsworth, famously. What does that mean? Seems to mean that at some point you had a big feeling, something blew your mind, and you're recalling it all of a sudden—like Proust with his Madeleine (my daughter's name, with the fancy French spelling for that very reason). It's spontaneous, it's happening to you, not so much *by* you, it's a possession, and it's still big, the feeling is, but it's not actually happening now, so you're remembering it but it's not overtaking you in quite the same way because you're tranquil now, you're just peacefully chewing a pastry, you're not freaking out like you were before, and yet there's still an overflow, there's still this kind of self-annihilation going on. A sublimity. A cordoning off of a trauma, whether beautifully or horridly scarring, within and behind the page. Okay, that's cool. I think I get something out of that, lotta back and forth—something seems familiar, there's a concept approaching understanding.

"Like a piece of ice on a hot stove the poem must ride on its own melting," according to Frost. Okay, that seems to me that a poem creates its own world, its own atmosphere and energy—it is its own wave, rides itself even as it disappears itself, even as it melts into oblivion, a phoenix rising from its own puddle. It is its own cosmos, has its own fiat lux, establishes each time out the standards by which it wishes to be judged, it creates and destroys itself in the same instant. Quite godly and self-destructive it is. But what could be more quintessentially human that that?

Let's run down a few more attempts at a definition. Frost again: "Poetry is what gets lost in translation." Yup. For Wallace Stevens, it was the "supreme fiction," replacing God on Sunday morning—a self-made source of morality even, through art and imagination rather than commandment. Well, a boy can dream. William Shakespeare loved to pun the equivalence between "nothing" and "noting," i.e., writing is nothing. And I don't think he protests too much. For T. S. Eliot, poetry "is not a turning loose of emotion, but an escape from emotion; it is not the expression of personality, but an escape from personality," and then he adds rather defensively, "But, of course, only those who have personality and emotions know what it means to want to escape from these things." Try posting that damnation of conformity masquerading as individuality on social media instead of some banal Billy Collins. I like this from Elizabeth Bishop: "What one seems to want in art, in experiencing it, is the same thing that is necessary for its creation, a self-forgetful, perfectly useless concentration." Useless and perfect, perfectly useless. How un-American and dangerous. Robert Lowell: "Poetry is not the record of an event: it is an event." Right. A muscular gloss on Wordsworth, I think. How do I know it's a poem? Let Emily Dickinson shine her strobe light on that—"If I read a book [and] it makes my whole body so cold no fire ever can warm me I know *that* is poetry. If I feel physically as if the top of my head were taken off, I know *that* is poetry. These are the only way I know it. Is there any other way?" One wishes Justice Dickinson had presided over James Joyce's obscenity trial.

I think I began writing poems to impress adults—my parents, people who admired books and writers, and, I think, my teachers as well, the people who taught me the words in the first place. It was my way of saying, *I'm listening, I'm learning, I'm taking it in, taking it to heart—don't kick me out, don't kill me, I'm one of you, one of the good ones.* The first book of poems I fell for was John Berryman's *77 Dream Songs.* And when I write, it is as tribute to what I received, and at the same time an attempt to forget that very thing. Trying to remember to forget my way back through to some original untaught, unworded state. As if any poem is an attempt to answer the ancient Zen koan: *Who were you before your parents were born?*

And then later, I suppose, I wrote to woo girls, to charm them with my wit and rhyme, my word music, because I didn't sing or play an instrument and a boy growing up on 11th Street and Second Avenue wasn't gonna be Mick Jagger. Maybe that's what Mick Jagger was doing. Maybe that's all a poet is ever doing. Freud would say that for sure—*It's sublima-*

tion, folks, the artist gets through art what he or she cannot get in life—the love of women/men, or whatever "other" one loves, and Uncle Siggy is the best literary critic we have; not the best therapist, but the best literary critic. All poems are love poems. Certainly not something to be proud of, the wooing of women and wisdom, but it has the ring of truth, and we must always listen for the ring of truth.

When I was in the PhD program in English literature at Yale, I studied with the capacious Harold Bloom, who summed up the notion of fame as being the hybrid child of our two great heritages—the Greek and the Old Testament Bible. Bloom said that the Greek notion of fame was horizontal—to be known far and wide across the globe (like a warrior or athlete) in the present moment, while the Hebrew notion of fame was vertical—to be known throughout time (like a warrior of thought). We poor offspring of this melded Western tradition are subjected to desiring both the horizontal *and* the vertical. I myself sought the horizontal through acting—courting worldwide fame in the here and now—while still harboring dreams of eternal verticality by writing my way into a future (without me) and thus conquering death. Both types of fame, spatial and temporal, belie a fear of death. I imagine writing for an unborn audience, my readers reanimating me when I am no longer here. A poem is like a possession of the reader, the poet's mind inhabiting the reader's mind, the dead poet's mind thinking the reader's mind, taking it over for a spell, and for a spell the poet lives again; eternity is possible. A type of zombie. All poems are poems about death. All poems are about love and death. So I've been scribbling poems to the idealized feminine and an imagined future for quite a while.

Yet at some point I did learn a musical instrument, and began to sing. I wanted more from my voice. And then I started writing lyrics. Lyrics are not poems. But they are in the same family. Cousins, maybe. A poem rides its own wave, a lyric rides the wave of music and melody. How does that work? Differently. There's way more rhyming happening. Rhymes that would seem cloying or trite on the bare page become lovely, even anticipated and deeply desired, in the chorus and verses. I am reminded of Umberto Eco: "Two clichés make us laugh. A hundred clichés move us." There is way less need to invent, to make it new; even moon-June clichés are welcome, because songs are democratic and unpretentious, they belong to everyone, to the folk, to other songs that came before. All songs are folk songs, and should strive for inclusion, not exclusion. Aphorisms work. "The love you take is equal to the love you make," "The Revolution Will Not Be Televised," "'Scuse me while I kiss the sky," "Mona Lisas and Mad Hatters"!—Nietzsche could've been a Bernie Taupin. Gnomic utterances work—"Break on through to the other side," "Different strokes for different folks," "You can't always get what you want, but if you try sometimes . . . you get what you need."

In a poem, the words are the words *and* the music. But a song rides the wave the singer sings before it; you have to leave room for the music just as the music must leave room for the lyrics. It's a fun dance. A cat-and-mouse game. And that was a new dance I discovered when I started writing songs.

A great lyric is not a great poem, and yet, and yet, lyrics have the undeniable merit of necessary restraint, the gorgeous limitations and humility of the form. And the mysterious pleasures and disciplines of rhyme. They have their own thing to offer.

But it is exactly that humble spirit of gorgeous limitations in which I offer these poems. The spirit of uselessness and beauty. The spirit of memory and forgetting and of thresholds honored and crossed. My deepest hope, one I'm a fool for saying out loud, is that they give you nothing of worldly worth and you can't get enough of them.

David Duchovny
6/1/25

Do Over

When you move, dark bits of your life
are shaken into light. A Polaroid, receipts
from a place you've "never been," a marble—
the midnight attic of your choices.
Such labels sink me like a stone
so I drive away with you
to "work on our relationship"
as naked as the law allows.

Still, the spiral narrows deeper in
flaying me of adjectives.
Being not myself confers strange powers,
only a couple of which
I ever discern.
But I can see at night. That's one.
All that is created
can be barely understood.
They say the big bang happened
when the devil told God to go fuck Himself.

Be that as it may,
I need to find a fiction
we can agree on.

This bridge,
this lonely crossing that I build for us.

You can't leave home
unless you have one.
And if your home is assembled poorly,
you will be defined

by what clings to you in your worst moments:
your anger your anchor.

It's freezing on the Avenue of the Giants.
The lightness
I thought would free me does no such thing.
Only desire returns me to a semblance,
only desire, like a tab of ecstasy,
stamps a smiley face on oblivion.
I worry your skin like a rosary.
Momentarily,
even the seals make sense and are in tune.
They sing: "As you learn, you teach."
The past suddenly seems
rife with possibility. In the future,
I shall let my wordless heart
do all the talking.

On the drive home,
I record the new names—
Arcadia, Eureka, Ukiah, and I remember
riding the LIRR when I was a kid,
hearing the magical spells chanted by the conductor—
Montauk, Patchogue, Massapequa—

And when the train sometimes slowed,
I imagined jumping off unseen between
stations and walking into these strange towns,
leaving my parents behind,
a ten-year-old city boy
knocking on a Long Island door, saying,
"I am a citizen of the world, take me, rename me;
I'll mow the lawn, do the dishes, wear the hand-me-downs,
whatever."

As each second passed, geography
would change my fate.
Every moment brought new towns, new families.
New lives.
Those were the days.

But I never did step off.
No, I don't think I ever did.

Carbon Canyon

We lived in Carbon Canyon then, before the fire,
unpack that given irony—were there no
carbon copies, we so unique and blessed?

There was a time when I walked
with my three-year-old daughter
(I think three . . .).
Anyway, I know we were walking the deep decline
of Carbon Canyon
on one of those short, mommyless jaunts . . .
And we came upon
the recently car-crushed carcass
of a gray field mouse, part three-dimensional
as in life,
part flattened as in a drawing,
the weight of the car
having made its lower half unreal, a cartoon.
The driver long gone,
unaware of their handiwork, guiltless.

A tiny trickle of blood from its slightly opened
mouth, a last profound unheard utterance,
so perfectly dramatic and telling
as if to seem placed by a movie crew
hiding in the bushes perhaps.

And my daughter (two, three, four?)
about to spy it on the ground, and I, a daddy,
with knowledge spilling out of my pockets,
life lessons, sense a teaching moment for the disquisition
on mortality that every parent believes

every three-year-old needs—
(see, it all ends, best laid plans and all that,
life's unfair; carpe diem, little one;
Latin for . . . heaven; there but for the grace of god—)
in these moments, I realize I am nothing but a recording
of my own parents' voices—their greatest hits,
my soul their phonograph . . .

Fade in: a father slows his daughter, allowing
the chance to happen upon a dead mouse,
it/death knowledge. Consequence. Mortality.
But it is only now, as we kneel,
that I notice the vibrant cha-cha line of ants
dancing in and out of the ruined creature
in all their anarchic discipline,
carrying to and fro unseeable bits of meat
and nutrient mouse ooze.

And my breath catches
because suddenly this lesson is for Daddy,
and it is Daddy who cannot face too much death,
the death after death, my death
in this mouse's mouth, my daughter's death.
I've not quite stomach enough
to face the pieces of us all carried off into oblivion,
eaten till we are unrecognizable, digested,
shit. Roadkill.

Dizzying, I say, "Oh, let's go, sweetheart . . ."

But it's too late—my daughter,
two or three or four, has seen,
leans down farther, her blue eyes
an inch or two from the ground, and says,

"Daddy, look, the ants, there's so many of them."
"Yes, I see. Maybe we should let the mouse sleep, let her sleep."

I take her hand to lead her, though I don't know where.
I know I am blind and unprepared,
a child leading a child,
and the little one stops and smiles,
and points back to the carnage—

"No, the ants, Daddy, the ants—look how much they love her."

Evergreen

The ancient mother sleeps not five miles
away, in a worry of dreams
she shutters over all times
except the present.
Unknown to herself, her body irksome
a source of no pleasures
only pains, her skin thin
and raw, slack her breath, and dry—
and yet her shame shades
the dying shoots of my love
hoarding the sun and rain
and is in me
evergreen.

Should've Listened to the Road

It said hazard reported up ahead
It said slippery when wet
It said men working in trees
It said yield
It said expect delays

It said no shoulder

Drive

My mind rushes in
like a fool
to fill any vacuum,
with specified night preferable
to no thing.
This relentless need to create, even a darkness visible,
or concrete fakes
built upon abstract mistakes—

Drive.

I saw a shape on the freeway
with the curves of an animal,
of life broken and bad-angled,
a deer, a dog, or person even.
I swallowed the air like broken glass,
shallowly, my heart went out, and approached
at the speed of light and limit,
the poor creature.

Turning my head quickly, I made out
not a deer or raccoon or living one,
but just a rug and/or tire or mattress
covered in debris, a shoe that could pass obliquely
for a shoulder, a pillow for a head,
a Something doubled over
to give the speeding appearance of depth,
of death and need
and form, and need,
arranged and shaken
by chance and careless drivers.

You know this phenomenon.

And all that lingered
was the rush of sympathy, my heart,
having reached out to meet this suffering thing,
still outside of me beating fast and a little embarrassed,
exposed.

And I thought:

Is that me
who passes for living?

And I thought:
Is that you, my absent friend,
who appeared to me in human disarray
but was just the imitation of life
off the side of some road?

No. No.
No. So, if no,
where is that road
where I can see you again
alive?

Where do I turn?
Or do I just face forward and

Drive?

Dead Seven

I don't need an occasion to think of my father occasionally,
dead now seven years.
Better than nothing, I hope waits
for him, an afterlife, a rebirth is it?
If so then, is the old man
young again in death?
A seven years dead-boy, growing steadily,
deadly, as he watches me in life grow?
Seven years learning the netherworld ropes,
still a child, by turns wide-eyed and sullen,
as he crawls, walks, runs,
into the walls of his newly unlimited understanding.
His seventy-five years or so on earth useless,
except as a dream of power, a moderately successful campaign
on tiny plastic soldiers.

Who is his mentor there? Who reminds him?
Who comforts him and teaches him
the otherworldly equivalent of fishing or algebra or
empathy for the dead living all around him?
Does he sit, dead little head in little dead hands,
on the curb, lonely and abandoned?
He who held my hands and taught
and did not teach
me so many things. Of nature and that nature—

I age like a tree, each new ring an orbiting armor
round an empty marrow: the things I did not learn
closed off at the center of my being, unreachable.
Of interest only to those who would chop me down to see
what I might deliver coldly from another age:

"Oh . . . so, you see here, this was the problem, right here.
The worm at the root, the uneven ring."

Older now in life than he in death,
I see him confused, reaching
for my steadying arm,
as a dead branch perjures life in the wind,
his language, his access to our symbols—
impenetrable, the dead tongue mute.
My need for him transcribed
into his imagined need for me;
my inarticulate want his.

Full fathom five, six,
seven, now going on eight,
my sweet sunken boy calls to me—

I am here,
I respond, *and ready,*
and of absolutely no use.

Moonrise

The earth's first love,
torn from his side as in Genesis,
the moon
fashioned from a rib of severed Eden.

Captivated in distant ellipses,
sometimes nearer, as often not,
no closer to breaking away than giving in.
A stasis of chaos.

Shadows cast upon each other, the shade
of lovers' discord, ancient enmities'
gist forgotten, lyrics lost; only remains
this music of the spheres.

Absent presence, she floats
on the airless air, changing shape
on monthly whim,
from full to bone.
She speaks to us in tides
and qualities of light,
and unfathomable loneliness.

She has her dark side.

Trapped by one another, in one another,
the same; there is no other
but this score that traces
zeroes upon the heavens,
endless nothings,
the ribbony symbol of infinity.

That original hurt, the violence
of some other body, that removed
the earth from itself, ourselves from ourselves,
cannot be fully known or overcome
fully. What's done is done but not gone,
if only by the sheer ungodly will
to remain in orbit
of something.

So the moon rises this morning,
pale and unimpressive in the California haze, gray,
fading chameleonic into its light-blue background,
like a shadow of last night's argument,
pulling water, the perversely named Pacific,
and our own watery flesh, upward
and closer, to the ever-ongoing
reconciliation of loss.

It Wasn't the Knife

Your mother helped me
with the disguise:
makeshift, a sheet, pantyhose over face,
a butter knife from the kitchen, whatever.
It was Halloween
and you were seven.

Crouching there in the dark, wondering
in future perfect regret
if this was a bad idea—
too much?
How was I to know
that it wasn't the knife—
that my hands and head were full
of a destruction more real
and lasting?

Confessions of a Pet Rock

I am not lazy or useless
or anyone's pet anything;
I am merely other.
I didn't want more
than to sit in my wordless be-ing,
my utter is-ness—
but if offered, I might have accepted another fate—

Thrown through that glass window, say, shattering
into a new dimension—
on the street alone, undomesticated by my fall,
dallying on my brother, the asphalt, waiting
for another hand to lend me the will,
momentarily, to raise me up,
in the face of my nemesis, captor, and lover—gravity;
which is my genius, waiting.
Then maybe used in a crime, say,
and called upon as witness
to the all-consuming play of your silly dramas:
a rock of importance.

Ah well, no regrets for me.

If only you could have slowed down to my time,
geologic,
the marking of years as milliseconds,
slower even than the evolutionary swell of ocean vowels
or the languid language of trees,
you might've learned something.

You might've learned the joke is on you.

Memory Palace

You must approach me as you would a ruin,
twisted logic riven in the stone.

The eccentric architecture whispers rumor
of trauma and whimsy,
semi-truths distorted echo in warping wood—
A ruination:
half designed by man, half by mad decay.

Memory replaces math as law.

The awful effects of time seem
almost purposeful; I own it.
I take credit.
This blueprint tossed together by
gravity, catastrophe, and will.

You ask for directions.
I may just give them.
That's when you should worry.
I may lie without meaning.
You may stand before a locked door
trying keys, codes, magic spells—waiting . . .
till another door creaks open behind you
into the Russian-doll floor plan of souls.
It's beginning to sound a little like
Abbott and Costello Meet the Wolfman—
(I won't deny my deepest influences).

This means nothing.
Sometimes you can just tell,

but other times you can't
as when darkness shines forth like light.
The circuitry is . . . circular,
every surface is reflective
like a shield.
The past looms ahead in a growing haze
of varying shades of sunset and gray;
the future lies behind me
like an invisible wake,
out of my sight, out of my mind.

Hybrid, shape-shifting, I do not
recognize myself in here.
I cannot be trusted, but
the haphazardry of it all . . .
maybe marvel at that,
the role of timing and luck and
what could have happened
but did not.
Original intent as lost as those of cave paintings;
it's all art, or artful,
simply as human as I can manage
on any given day.

This is love's warning:

My father's house has many rooms
and I have room and time for many more,
room and time so far.

Do not be unafraid.

Paper Beats Rock

Since you said you'd stay a month,
and stayed three hours;
I've not been entirely committed. Just
my heart
went on the lam, a soft fugitive,
hanging so low
in the Starbucks parking lot,
saying he's at the office, a decaffeinated criminal,
my heart stole a muffin, bums change with a hard luck sign
at Hollywood and Vine, dials long-extinct 212 numbers,
shoots foul shots alone, compares notes with no one,
my heart
watches porn at the Hollywood Hawaiian Hotel,
beats over fast,
gets disgusted with itself and overeats,
sips tequila through a vein he calls a straw;
kid's stuff, victimless crimes in a tepid time,
but enough for the Authority
to take note.

So—they want to commit my heart upstate
for observation. Who's zooming who,
you may rightly ask. But they're looking for
my heart
with a cute little Jarvik straightjacket.
My heart
in a fist-sized trench coat, smoking a cigarette like an artery,
on a nostalgic trip, watching carefree kids at a local
schoolyard,
a sad small man,
trying to find the beat that she skipped to,

then skipped like a broken record,
then skipped like a stone
on the water out of town.

There, with his left ventricle pressed
against the fence unbored, watching infinite games
of rock paper scissors shoot, the Authority finds my heart
and places him under cardiac arrest,
shipping him asap upstate in a valentine's-shaped ice chest—
where he is committed entirely, takes pills with meals,
bpm within target range, writes me in crayon
from a mandatory art class, requesting
his black and blue cardigan,
misses me, misses her,
writes poems halfway through,
and dedicates them to cities he's never been to,
my heart
plotting his return to a world diminished
by her ineradicable presence.

Dragnet Spec

You say to get at truth:
strip the thing down to the bare act,
the fact of what happened, context
is bullshit, excuses, tell me
the nouns, leave out the adjectives, description.
You distrust art everywhere it might count
for something, art is like extra credit
without getting credit.
Acts is numbered in the Bible, yes,
ABC and so on, causality is a dodge
to you, life is numbered and color-coded,
gray is not among those colors.

I sound defensive.
Dismissive.
Crafty.
And guilty.

Let's start over.
Good choice of words? :)
As in can we?
:(
Sorry . . . the thing was done.
I did the thing, yes,
period. The thing was did.
I did the thing period.
The thing has no story, the thing has no context,
the thing is the thing.
Getting better doesn't mean all better now.
Playing with words again, like a child, like a
child who is squirming around for mercy.

Grown-ups are not distracted by story,
grown-ups do not care for shiny things
like birds do.
Birds and children.
Grown-ups are like the cops on *Dragnet*:
"Just the facts, ma'am."
Here's the thing, sir, just tell me
the what not the how
it happened.
It happened, yes?
Say it simply, so we can agree on something.
The thing happened, the heart broke.
Wait, that's metaphor, that's context,
the heart cannot
really break.
Oh yes, the heart is the heart
is a muscle and therefore
it can tear, rip, break even, not quite like a bone,
but very much like a bone.
Be satisfied with that.
But that's a figure of . . .
No, that is fact of not figure of.
Shit, there's a page missing.
No matter,
No matter? Once again,
it happened, yes?
Yes, but . . .
Okay, shhhh . . . doesn't that feel better?
No but . . .
Sssssssshhhhhhhhhhhh . . . end of the story.
And stop complaining,
you could've played Joe Friday
but you didn't, you wanted the showy bad guy role,
that was your choice, vanity.

But bad guys go away,
to other shows,
or stop working altogether,
Friday works every week.
That is literally true, a fact,
and people say TGIF, don't they?
They do.
Friday makes the week make sense.
Maybe you lost sight of that ;(
Fact.
Do I get a lawyer?
Ohhhhhhh yes you do!
Whoa, a duck just dropped from the sky! :0
An omen? Maybe this is wrong . . .
Hardly, you said the magic word is all.
Finally.
But that's another show, the spin-off,
that's a whole 'nother story:

You'll need a pen for this.

Ridley's Stanzas to 'Rona

One

Now is the silent spring of our discontent,
what is said seduces what is meant.
The breath of life is lethal—
we have nothing to fear but fear itself,
oh yeah, and other people:
I've got a lot to say and nothing to do,
there's a gun in my mouth, but it's pointed at you.

Two

The Siren's songs are now our saviors,
reminding us to modify our behaviors.
Tie yourself to the mast and mask:

$<6'=6'$ *under*
(that's the *new* new math)

Three

Okay, let's make it a game, kids, remember how to play
keep away—
and stay, please baby baby, please stay
the fuck away from me.

The wicked witch has cast her hex:
"Six shall take the place of sex."

Four

A record year and yield,
a world rebranded as a hotter potter's field.
Raccoons stroll down shuttered Columbus,
and snide Riverside rejoices at our troubles.
Ol' foxy Chaos smugly walks among us
breaking windows and chatting amiably with the locals.
Everything and nothing is the same.
I hear pigeon spoken on Madison and rumors rampant
of a ratty bear down on Wall Street
juggling algorithms and popping shiny real estate bubbles.

The Hudson forgets its name
as Central Park
gets down to work
on an Ark.

Five

I know you want to adventurously roam,
but these days, even Homer has to stay at home.
Every subway, bus, and cab is a poisoned chalice;
so, for the foreseeable future,
It's *Uber über alles.*

And if you don't like this movie,
all things being unequal,
seems the powers that be hit a wall on the sequel:
the broken air's a crown of thorns,
but Christ Knows Best:
you must die before you get reborn.
Selves themselves are shelved

and shelves are empty,
fears are found and founded,
planes and dreams aground and grounded.

Birds fill the vacated sky
Finally finally finally free to fly.

Six

I've lost all sense
of what it takes to mend
the hearts and minds, the ties that bind,
the broken towers, the recompense
of unremarked hours—
I fear I fear I fear, I ken
we are out of time,
for every discordant thing chimes and rhymes
with death.
The words themselves and world are sick and tired
of the world of men:

The fevered planet shivers and turns
a cold shoulder to our pleas,
then shakes us off like fleas.

Heads or Tails

I

The house inside me is dark.
They are asleep, or out, or dead. The past.
The key is not under the mat, no windows are open
a crack. I am locked out
from what I was.
So I take a picture;
it'll last longer.
I am a photographer of such deathly moments
from which I make zombies, and sometimes money.
Do you have a pose for me?

II

Most ancient camera lucida, my soul,
accepts her imprint like the primitive machine it is.
I cannot break her to pieces—
eyes, hair, pussy, *joie*—
tear her limb from limb in the name of love, cannot
but also cannot endure the whole of her,
not ready for God to ram His tongue down my throat.
I am stuck outside
in the windswept street, a passport snapshot yellowing
in my wallet, busted on the ground, kneeling
before a statue of limitations.

III

To make the inside outside is the key.
To notify the folks of a change in my address,
I throw a rock through the window and prowl
long-forgotten corridors, inhaling primal odors

of cat, Lysol, brussels sprouts—hearing the old
silver radiator hissing and clanking like a sinking ship,
and my own small self, and my brother, conspiring amid
the enamel, beard rubs, and unlockable doors, I realize—
I am looking for a wife.

IV

In the bedroom I expect to see my mother crying.
For in memory, as in visions of hell,
we are fated eternally to the definitive gesture.
We are subjected to the shorthand of the master—
thus this one reclines ambiguously.
Thus this one runs from first to third.
Thus my mother cries.
Her hand-muffled moans gently shake the creaking bed,
working the metal wheels into the wooden floor in
a calligraphy of marriage—half desperation,
half fruitful fucks.
The sadness and sex
that created me spinning two impossible halves
into one unstable identity—
head over heels, heads or tails, heads and/or tails,
those conversant with tragedy have trouble
choosing sides.
Sides are chosen still.
But this is not my mother.

V

It is my father, not crying.
Not crying for all he's done,
not crying for all he hadn't done,
for all he always will and will never do,
not crying.
I lift him up on my shoulders, like a dime-store Aeneas;

he is surprisingly light, as if carved from balsa wood,
as weightless as the man in the moon.
Nietzsche says—angels can fly because they take themselves
so lightly.
I fly the coop.

VI

Out of that weeping house at last,
on Second Avenue now, I look up at my father
riding piggyback on me,
and it is not my father. It is you,
my wife, long estranged, never met.
You disembark me.
We stand on level ground.
I see an old couple leaning on each other for support.
Two pigeons fly off wing to wing, the world
pairing up in unnoticed omens, real history
is unrecorded.

VII

Your hands slide into my patched pockets of memory
in a gesture lovers somehow know,
but you find them filled with coins—
quarters, Kennedy half-dollars,
pesos, shekels, doubloons, Buffalo head nickels,
mercury dimes, ancient Roman coins—
the currency of the world,
a pocket history of man's desire
to store his potential in shiny immutable metal, and you,
you toss them in the air, smiling like
you've pulled them from behind my ear, and I,
I cannot choose which is more enchanting—
the sun breaking on the gold, silver, and copper,
or the ringing notes as they hit the sidewalk:

a magician's trick.
I am home with you out in the street,
paralyzed upon the precipice
of all I have been given, all I have lost, and
all that remains—
all of existence here, above and below us,
heads tails heads tails heads tails:

They called Jesus a magician too.

City of Los: Population: 1

You gotta admit
The one thing you can't omit
The obit—

May I add, I would've liked to have been
more or less
driven. But—

This paperweight, my heart,
steadies pages of the past
against a wind of change;
it's insane what you could have had—
so light now the breeze takes it.

Leaving Los Angeles

Here there is always someone else.
Something else. Somewhere else.
There is always another answer,
and like dated milk, good for only so long,
a season or two. Maybe.

Your container will be filled yearly, monthly,
daily, and you will rise in the morning
as empty as a slice of blue sky in the uncanny valley.
You will cry, sure, you want to be tucked into
consciousness like a prefab piece, and it's true,
everything you see whispers of satisfaction—

Cars seem to wanna fuck you.

Clothes seem to wanna fuck you.

Music seems to wanna make you as young
as when you first heard it, and then fuck you.

So you forget your way back—
leaving all this on a beat that says:
There is no leaving this.

A Dream

You dreamt you wrote something so good,
so ambivalent and destructive, so creative,
so lacking in morals or decency, or instruction,
so sad and so funny,
so useless and old,
so familiar and new,
so full of theft and power

that they had to name a god after it.

When you woke,
the page of your mind was bare
and the world was changed.

Down with Love

One year past per second per second chance
waves of feeling mind distinctive chemical tides,
FKA "moody"; tied to the postnatal gravity
of some psychic black hole, invisible,
having crushed matter into a flat slab
of lost time, sucking all that dared
near it into school uniform gray matter
hardly matters—
I could toy with labels and syndromes and dime-store
causality, sophistry, tapestry,
but in the end, all there is is
ineffable intransigence.
There, I nailed it.

With my own gravity
of purpose, a new form has risen, a new moon
calling on a child's walkie-talkie
to her ancient lover to meet for dinner or dancing
or ever.
From a distance, everything looks small and unhurried.
The moon is no Darwinian, and my heart swings
to the lunar lover's law tonight.
Fifty beats per second per second squared,
accelerating in minutes to ostensible infinity.

What holds the planets in alignment
is love and weight. What lathes the sea
to the land is love and repetition. What makes
my soul captive to my body is love
and fate, and what breaks me apart
like a wave upon a rock is love

for you—giving expression in the moment of destruction
bound so tightly, I am suddenly capable
of generosity. I am free to toy loosely
with universal laws, physics is for poets
to play with until they die;
just as I
gladly succumb to those selfsame laws,
growing old old old and down down
down with love.

Rest in Peace, Fred Hellerman

Now the men my father's age,
born the year he was, are dying fast,
my father already long dead.
Luck no longer plays a part,
nor his iffy heart.

No broccoli or coffee,
no swimming or embrace of the pillow
over a night on the town,
what made the man a particular man:
his choices to stay
or leave, who to love and who not to,
dwindle to not meaning
as all fall down and back and
multicolored fate fades to black.

And yet, my own being, molded by
the undocumented vagaries of his willing
or not willing, forever now lost—
keeps invisible score,
and always wants always
wants more.

New Haven

The first time in your little apartment, a small bedroom,
maybe claustrophobic, not feeling worthy, overcome by
your presence and ease and point of view, making excuses
for finishing fast and all but begging for another shot,
which you so kindly gave me.
Stopping by to see you on my way from NYC
to a wedding in New England, you
being the only person I knew who stayed in New Haven for
the summer.
A lovely hot no-AC kinda day.
You, always so good tempered and kind and supple and the
sex
as you say—even.
A draw, a tie. A hammock? Inside?
Did a squirrel not give birth to babies on your sill?
Little blots of gray/pink like discarded bubble gum,
the mommy howling like an animal many times her size.
A couple at some grad school party where some weird guy
and his pretty girlfriend
wanted to go to bed with us.
She had a Nordic name and he I actually ran into
on a street by UCLA a few years ago.
You would be pleased to know
he is a psychoanalyst, of course.
He had begun by talking to me in the showers of Payne
Whitney:
I thought he was interested in my mind.
An awkward night at my mother's where we slept on a single
bed.
This could have been the last night.
Many other moments of your strong simple goodwill—

late-night phone calls or emails through the decades,
as regular as an eclipse—
a flare, here and there, from ship to ship.
Certain slips and rebounds, the exact feel of you remains present
to this day for reasons only something knows,
but thank you for all that.
Friend.

How Does It Go?

I call upon the ghost of us
to haunt us.

Individually, we leave behind no corpse
full enough to demand an entire body.
I am a hand that caresses and a foot in a mouth, you
a run of cock-hardening belly and hair
and the clearest of eye and intention.
In the blender of death, of scrambled argument, stretched
over time until it resembles nothing
but a story badly told,
a joke ruined at the punch line
by a faulty setup—

Wait, did I mention there were two priests and a rabbi?
Let me start again. So.

And yet together, these maimed souls,
sanded and grooved like sea glass
by decades of sleeping side by side
in the back and forth of the ocean bed,
form a one.
Assembled from the frankensteinian bits
in a cartoon whirlwind of joint creation
into this thing,
this creature,
that is more terrifying when gone
than when not.

We do not recognize our own
And so our own disowns us.

Who was I all this time? The countless nights
of easy silence or jangly unspokenness,
and who were you, safe in your neutral corner,
neither rocking the boat nor taking your hand
off the tiller?

Can what is not dead be reborn?
Wait, that's not the end,
let me start over . . . A dog walks into a bar . . .

The invisible stepchild, the other, the monster,
cobbled-together scraps of who we were
in the beautiful mutual incompleteness
of our togetherness,
roams this B-movie countryside
bereft and bereaving me,
still unformed yet again,
like an overly made-up Olivier,
too old to be young and too young to be old,
a Heathcliff whisper/yelling *Haunt me*
to our apparition.

How does it go now?
In less exalted terms, tell me,
exactly when do you give up the ghost?

We've traced the calls, Mrs. So and So,
they're coming from inside the house.
Funny that. Hold on.
Let me try once more.
From the beginning this time
with feeling—

A man and a woman meet, fuck,
no,
how does it go again?

Hope you're god . . .

The text ended from the woman
who was his wife
in another life.
It had been full
of cheery news of shared children
and mostly forgotten mutual friends
who once upon a time
had chosen sides
and custodized
like kids in a playground pickup game.
Recriminations faded to mere whiffs
or paranoid riffs,
like her use of the word "bill" for money
momentarily sent him down the road
of who the fuck is/was Bill to her?
(O my love, what happened?
Will we ever know
why we chose to narrow so
and let it go?)
It ends, as all things must,
with a form of goodbye
and a typo.
Having no time, maybe,
to read for errors,
or maybe amused
at her own wayward thumbs
(still trying to get in her head, jesus, stop).
"Hope you're god"
was what she wrote.
Like an old wish
half remembered

from a halo of auditioning wishes
over a birthday cake,
a moment before eight
candles were blown dark.
(O my love, my old dear, my lost cause)

Hope you're god too.

Nobodaddy Home

The hole in my heart is emptied out.
He is gone for good,
the one who left so long ago.
Whom I chased through women and success,
lounging like a roman à clef
above this restlessness,
collecting attributes like dried leaves,
phone calls, sugar-covered memories—
it is not the hole that hurts,
but what you put in it, how you fill it,
the grade-school grammar of your loss.
And what is left is a whiff
of emptiness, past tense, italicized,
as irrelevant as that old man on a plane
back to gay Paris. As I, too,
become beside the point to myself, free,
doomed to start again, playing chicken
with oncoming identities,
learning lines, scratching lines to try to make sense
of unmarked ground.

High-Five the Sky

When everything is permitted, our dreams will cease
in the bright daylight of lukewarm acceptance.
Sleep becomes impossible,
shadows a thing of the past—
replaced by shallows.
Lighter still, we have traded something away
that remains to be seen;
and we will wander the easy streets
high-fiving the sky imbecilically,
unbeknownst to ourselves
mourning wanly the badlands,
our old mythic difficulty.

We cannot know how good for us
the bad times were.

As the Crow Flies

The shortest distance

the straight line.

                When the fuck

                              has that ever happened?

Cupid

What I want to know is
what idiot
gave that fucking blind kid
a bow and arrow?

Hardcover

A weekend, not even,
time away from time,
driving lightless at night, our eyes no more
than two seconds ahead of our flesh
down the road.

I can't sleep.

So I read.

To distract myself.

Of men who are sadder, lonelier, more brave
than me.
And women who are not as beautiful
or as funny as you.
I reach for an unfamiliar hard
cover, its spine uncracked.

And when I open, find whole
chapters ripped out by the handful,
pages and pages torn as if by some mad editor,
or censorious librarian, or jealous god.
Impossible to make out a story
or follow a thread—

Something about kissing,
then the rest is missing.

Future Perfect

A sound (what is that?) reminds me
of (what? I don't know). These days
there is so much familiarity with something
I have no experience of. Like the internets or
whatever. As if—
I passed you on 77th and Broadway
decades ago, and you smiled at me
for no (every) reason, laughed even,
then nothing (nothing?)
till now.
Et tu?
The future perfect,
insinuating into our momentarily
narrowed quotidian-like heavenly rust,
or a dumb hunch,
some beautiful-ass nonsense,
or the starting up again
of what has never been.

Professional Demon

The old demons these days,
not what they used to be, call me
by pet names, their fondness
barely hidden beneath perfunctory hostility.
I know for a fact a certain childhood Terror
that literally yearns to make me dinner.
But like cartoon nemeses, they are fixed;
Coyote must chase Roadrunner;
it's in his nature and in the script.

These days I see Coyote at the bar, slapping
that annoying fucking bird on the tail like a teammate,
buying drinks all around, toothless, the Acme handbook,
unattended in his back pocket, laughing at all the old
indignities, cataloging the injuries, the falls,
the explosions in his face as if
they are tattoos, not scars,
art, not violence.
But in his eyes, only a fool would deny
a shimmer of the old chaos, so

I sometimes commit the sin of forgetting
the possibility that dreams, daydreams, stray thoughts,
still have gain of function, can still
open up doors to old worlds, introduce the old gods
into the vacuum.

Drunk, at two a.m., and rabid, Coyote
manages a first howl in years and wonders:

Where the fuck have I been?

A bloody feather
floats to earth
like my complacent heart.

LA's a Bad Place to Die

with its ironic sunlight on the day of your passing.
Its improbable frost on a winter's summer morning,
completely forgotten, like you, by midday,
when the mercury hits eighty.
The once-hoped-for narrative of your life,
the celluloid cuttings on a Friday floor,
swept by Santa Ana into a keystone sequence,
a horror of nonsense,
a one-in-a-million shot,
that what's remembered or assembled by chaos
will provoke a laugh or a tear,
find an arc,
a hedge,
against projected eternity.

A tale edited by an idiot,
full of surround sound and fury,
dignifying nothing.

The parched desert plain
mistakes your blood for rain,
and the rest is science.

Long-Shot Man

Long shot: man alone
Close-up: beautiful woman turns, surprised
Close-up: man smiles—
he knows something

Dolly across bedroom, two silhouettes make love (discrete)
Long shot: garden, a wedding—
pan across guests, feeling of joy,
sloppy singles of parents, alcohol, bad funny dancing

Two shot: man and woman kiss, widen out
rise to blue sky on the move ('60s zoom?)

Hard cut to—
Medium shot: doctor holds up baby, push in on baby
(innocence/hope/worry)
Montage—more babies, pets, laughter, elections, houses,
funeral, ocean, etc.

Cross-fade—
Long shot: man, troubled, push in, shakes his head
Close-up: woman looking off,
she feels something—we don't know
Extreme close-up: her tear.
(Cheesy? Probably. Who cares?
Don't be afraid of the cheese.)

Cut wide to maybe a sun setting or the full moon,
a photo in a broken frame?—
something that tells us something . . .
pushing in feels like change happening . . .

ominous music . . .
Hard cut—

Master—city street (Toronto for New York)
A moving van pulls away (rain would be nice and/or wind)
Stay wide, two/three kids on the street wave goodbye, backs
to us
Close-up: man driving, unreadable
Close-up: woman, unreadable
Music over—
Fade out
The end

Cliché Juice

Home is where the heart is, and my heart is
traveling.
Up into the wild blue yonder, praying
this miracle of flight will not end, just yet.
But I am also at home with you, grounded
like a teenager, like a wire, like a bird and a wire,
feet on the ground, heart in my throat,
descending with gravity to the lower,
lowest, most sought after, most beautifully bound, home.

Aspirations involve reparations.
We reach for the stars wondering where we are.
But reason has been found by finding you
and looking down.

And it is down here—not in the stars
of fantasized worlds, fifth dimensions, or holy
parallel potentates of potentialities—that my feet will trace
their dance, slow as history.
A walking calligraphy so subtle, it'll take
decades to decode.

This mythical beasty—itinerant stasis,
and a lofty remove
to read the cursive strokes of aggregate footsteps,
like a fairy-tale dissolve,
once or twice upon a time—
engraved upon this little plot
of earth. Wherever
our home will be, wherever
we happen to be.

Gratitude

Thank you for the hole in my heart,
I spackled in the cracks with art.
Thank you for the needle in my arm,
I gilded it with childish charm.
Thank you for the pillow by my head,
for which I stole the down from strangers' beds.
A bullet in a pearl-chambered gun,
the honeyed fuck you that is me,
any mother's son.

Another Brick

I put my dog down this morning
and cried some, mourning
the loss of his mute expressive soul.
This afternoon, at work, a blue sky
punctuated only by disjointed loitering clouds—
the world moves on in its blithe way
and doesn't care
about a little dog—
it's already as if he never existed:
But he did.
He sure did.

Ah, Cleverness!

Ah, Cleverness, you old fool,
skimming across the ocean's skin
like a stone thrown by a boy—
where can I lose you?
Where can I lose?

What is this darting to a shiny thing?
A seduction of me by myself,
a demonstration to myself and others,
that I still got it. Got something anyway—
it, id, ID.
A safe word for joy,
more like a tombstone, a marker
for lightning strikes and absence
that may or may not exist, or
have existed or always will.
Here lies: enthusiasm.
Here: lies.
So, love. Strip—
strip away, keep stripping away
until nothing is left but divine presence,
until nothing is left but presence,
until nothing is left.

Do I mistrust it, or
is it the sole thing I trust?
More and more, it seems a defense,
a flair flare in the dark,
a nanny in the night, but
against what?
Age death ego irrelevance.

Look at me—still playing past dinner,
still skipping flat rocks above the blue-black depths,
"carefree" as an orphan,
as if I have nothing else to do,
nowhere else to be;
play on, child, keep believing
that the piper pipes for your pleasure,
that all this is for you
and not for what is due.

You always imagined
you were meant to go deeper, always
in training, your lungs and receptors,
for the other world.
It was the justification for your ornery solitude,
and though you were really gone elsewhere,
you never really "went there"—
knowing in the blueprint of your mind
that this was Kafka's door
that you waited outside for,
meant for only you,
and the sole way it swings is in,
in swinging shut;
you shall know thyself by where you cannot let yourself go.

There is no aha,
only haha.

No, you never quite got there, did you?
What lies beneath,
in sublime shapes inhospitable to meaning,
crouching, waiting to strike,
with annihilating maw.
Thine not mine the power
and the glory.

Skim upon the surfaces like a mayfly,
a winged rainbow, soon is June,
you gorgeous gadfly
in the mouth of a terrible lizard,
ah!

Homesick for Mystery

Sometimes it feels like yesterday.
Sometimes it feels like another lifetime.
Sometimes it feels
like it never happened.
Is love then how death loses itself?
Or is death how love does?

I must forget, I mean
I realize I must remember
to forget.
Not trying to be funny or clever—
but forgetting is not complete
outside of the movie plot, that is delusion.
Could it be amnesia is the ultimate fantasy?
Greater even than eternity or infinity.

In practical terms,
more like a mnemonic vaccination
should be developed,
the root of which, we forget, comes from cows:
a small inert dose of the pain, cordoned off,
memorialized but not enlivened, a little death,
the body alerted but unharmed,
the mind the same, but not—
obliquely empowered, lighter, unencumbered—
the only way forward
out of fury.

One day soon,
science will explain all that.
Science will explain everything,

and that is the day,
liberated and doomed,
we will forget what we have forgotten
and, homesick for mystery,
nostalgic for the ancient thundering binary
and its easeful certainty,
its comforting hum of prehistoric technology,
we will believe everything
and believe in nothing.

God Is a Changed Man

We read much
of how God changes men,
of how women change men,
of how children change men.
We read much of how men change,
or the other story—
of how they don't.

But I think maybe God can change, too.
I think maybe God is change.

How confused must God be,
how misunderstood in His heaven,
as He sees the numberless houses
built to honor His son,
and His word—
They don't get Me, He thinks,
they just don't get Me.
The death of My son, oh,
the skinny boy's long suffering on the cross,
his sense of shame—
(I imagine him wondering how
the son of God could be brought so low—the kid
must feel like it's his fault somehow)—this memory—
always sits with My son, even to this day,
as he sits with Me—
I see it behind his eyes,
though he will not say.
And how can I assuage his pain?
What can I say?
It was meant to be?

I fucking hate that.

Why would I want to be reminded
by all these spires
reaching up to touch Me, itching
at My celestial robes?
Why can't we be allowed to forget?
I and Thou.

Forgetting is the holiest of holies, but
My eternal mind does not come by this change
easily. Sadly,
I can remember everything
I've ever done,
which is everything.
Imperfection implies change. That I,
of all things, change
proves My imperfection then,
and conversely, hints at
my increasing perfection now.
It's really true what that guy Paul said:
truth surpasses understanding.
I paraphrase.

I look forward to the day
when the acts of man
outnumber Mine.
Dream on, you say.
It's easy for You to say, you say, easy
for the people to say, I say,
when I always hear them saying:
Jesus was Me.
Jesus was My soul incarnate.
Jesus was My gift—all this,

more and more, merely inflicts more,
opens old wounds—
how the fuck can I heal?

And the people don't get it.
It's like they want Me to feel good,
but I swear these elaborate formulae
and equations to square us Three into One
—listen,
the map is not the territory,
the territory always remains
incognita,
even when steepled and peopled.

And don't even get Me started on the Holy Spirit,
that slippery cat.
The Holy Spirit is the wild card,
the Holy Spirit is the game changer,
the Holy Spirit
is the spirit of forgetting.
She is not Me but She is of Me.
Deal with it.

They don't know—strike that,
they refuse to know—
that I am not the same God as before
I dabbled myself
into this world of pain
(which I seem unable to forget I created).
I am not where I was
nor am I yet where I will be
because I am everywhere;
I am also nowhere
but I am here now

always.
If you seek Me, I vanish—
it's a tic of Mine,
I'm working on it.

These people,
they're fucking everywhere,
they squeeze into my hiding places,
they don't know that they are
praying to a dead star.

And the father in Me fears
that that is not good
for either of us.

I Say No

I sit and wait for the words to come.
Not those words.
Cleaner words,
words untarnished by experience, by reality.
Words coming straight from the unnameable,
from the I am that I am.
Slim chance and none.

I sit and wait for the magic moment
that I have nothing to say.
I say yes to this and no to that.
I say no.
Skeptical of beauty and rhyme, adjectives,
wary of metaphor and comparison
pulling at the tether of dirty daily self.
A fool in a fool's game.
I know it cannot happen—
this daydream of pouring myself directly into you
by pouring myself directly into me,
a fantasy of wise and ineloquent innocence.
Fat chance.

I sit and wait by banishing thoughts of you
and you and you
and what you might make of me
and me and me.
Levels upon levels of interference,
of strategy, marketing, marking, and mist;
the horizon where memory bleeds into forgetting—
that primal residue, that holy outline.
I say no.

I sit and wait till I am lost.
I sit and wait till I give up
and go about the deadly detailed day.
But still, I wait for the words to come.
I do not yet have nothing to say.
Not those words, I say.

opens
One door ~~closes~~

closes
Another door ~~opens~~